GET ACTIVE!

EXTREME SPORTS

Barbara C. Bourassa

Copyright © QED Publishing 2007

First published in the UK in 2007 by
QED Publishing
A Quarto Group company
226 City Road
London EC1V 2TT
www.qed-publishing.co.uk

A catalogue record for this book is available from the
British Library.

ISBN 978 1 84538 746 4

Written by Barbara C. Bourassa
Edited, designed and picture researched by
 Starry Dog Books Ltd
Consultant Steven Downes, of the Sports Journalists'
 Association www.sportsjournalists.co.uk

Publisher Steve Evans
Creative Director Zeta Davies
Senior Editor Hannah Ray

Printed and bound in China

Website information is correct at time of going to press.
However, the publishers cannot accept liability for any
information or links found on third-party websites.

All the sports in this book involve differing degrees of
difficulty and the publisher would strongly advise that
none of the activities mentioned is undertaken without
adult supervision or the guidance of a professional coach.

Words in **bold** can be found in
the Glossary on pages 30–31.

Picture credits
S = Shutterstock.com, C = Corbis,
D = Dreamstime.com, G = Getty Images,
BSP = Big Stock Photo.com,
ISP = iStockphoto.com, F = Fotolia.com

t = top, b = bottom, l = left, r = right, c =
centre, FC = front cover, BC = back cover

FC (main image) G/ © Philip & Karen
Smith, (top to bottom) ISP/ © Brent
Deuel, D/ © Isoft123, D/ © Partyof7infl,
courtesy of the National Dutch Scooter
(Footbike) Federation, F/ © Jarvis Gray,
F/ © Eric Foltz, F/ © Nicholas Rjabow.
BC D/ © Ijansempoi.

1 D/ © Ijansempoi; 4 S/ © Putchenko
Kirill Victorovich; 5 (top to bottom) F/
© Jarvis Gray, F/ © Eric Foltz, F/ ©
Nicholas Rjabow, F/ © dogbone66;
6t C/ © Elmar Krenkel/Zefa, 6b C/ ©
Martin Philbey/ZUMA; 7 (main image)
C/ © Al Fuchs/NewSport; 8b courtesy
of the National Dutch Scooter (Footbike)
Federation; 9t D/ © Vangelis; 9b C/ ©
LWA- JDC; 10b G/ © Ryan McVay; 11t
G/ © Michael Kelley; 11 (main image)
D/ © Kineticimagery; 12t (left to right)
S/ © Peter Weber, S/ © Shawn Pecor,
S/ © Byron W.Moore; 12b S/ © Lavigne
Herve; 13 (main image) G/ © Philip
& Karen Smith, 13b courtesy of IMBA-
UK; 14b D/ © Godfer; 15t S/ © Nick
Poling, 15b C/ © Stuart Westmorland;
16–17 courtesy of Gomberg Kites; 17t
G/ © Karl Weatherly; 18t G/ © Jump
Run Productions, 18b © Drew Brophy;
19 G/ © Warren Bolster; 20t courtesy
of Connelly Skis; 20b C/ © Elizabeth
Kreutz/NewSport; 21t ISP/ © James
Boulette, 21 (main image) ISP/ © Brent
Deuel; 22t C/ © Nawang Sherpa/
Bogati/ZUMA, 22b G/ © Zigy Kaluzny;
23 G/ © Ryan McVay; 24b C/ © James
L. Amos; 25t C/ © Ariel Skelley, 25b
D/ © Isoft123; 26 courtesy of Teresa
Nightingale, www.attentiondesign.ca; 27l
F/ © Serge Simo, 27r © Meghan Lapeta;
28t courtesy of www.usaswimming.org/
Sara McLarty and family, 28b G/ ©
David Madison; 29 G/ Mike Powell.

CONTENTS

THE TERM 'extreme sport' means many things to many people. For children, however, it usually means cutting-edge sports such as skateboarding, surfing, IronKids (**triathlon**) and mountain biking. The term became widely used from 1995, when the US television sports channel ESPN launched the Extreme Games (later changed to the **X Games**), an international competition for more unusual, exciting sports.

Trendy, but not new!

Most of the extreme sports in this book have a modern reputation, but some have been around for a very long time. Surfing and kiting, for example, are actually thousands of years old. Rock climbing as a sport dates from the 1880s, while mountain biking and kneeboarding are child-friendly versions of adult sports (motocross/BMX and waterskiing).

▶ Rock climbing is a bit like learning to ride a bike, in that once you have learned the basics, you'll never forget them!

INTRODUCTION

PROTECTIVE GEAR

You'll notice that people who you see climbing vertical rock faces, performing 'ollies' in a skate park or kayaking down rushing rivers always wear protective gear. You'll usually see them with a helmet, pads, ropes, life jackets and the like. The right kit is important because many extreme sports lift you into the air, and wearing protective gear around your head and body can prevent injuries when you come back down to earth. As the proverb says, 'What goes up, must come down'!

Learning the basics

As any good **coach** will tell you, learning a new sport means understanding and mastering the basics. You'll need to look after your equipment carefully, do lots of practice and make sure you have expert help. All sports keep you healthy and active. So, remember to drink plenty of water, eat well and take breaks whenever you need to, whether you're running a race, cycling a trail or kayaking down a river.

Keep safe

Photographs of extreme sports are often exciting and fun to look at, but the children or adults pictured are usually very experienced and many will have been practising for years. They may also be using expensive, specialized equipment. Don't expect to be able to make the same moves straight away. However, you can expect a fun and exciting time if you put safety first – so turn the pages and get the low-down on a range of exhilarating extreme sports!

SKATEBOARDING

SKATEBOARDING dates from the 1950s. Many sport experts say the first skateboards originated in California, where the sport of surfing met the sport of roller-skating. This resulted in the invention of a long, flat board with four fat wheels attached. To get a skateboard moving, you stand on it with one foot, and push it along with the other. Once your speed is up, you can glide along with both feet on the board.

FIX IT YOURSELF!

Many children repair their own skateboards using specialized tools. The wheels of a skateboard sometimes wear out, and the surface of the board may need repainting with a fresh new design.

What's an 'ollie'?

An 'ollie' is a common skateboarding move in which the skateboarder steps down on the back of the board as he or she is going along in order to lift up the front and 'get air'. It is named after Alan "Ollie" Gelfand, a world-famous skateboarder from California.

Skateboarders often wear specially designed shoes with shock-absorbing heel pads and flat rubber soles that grip the board well.

THE RIGHT GEAR

When you are skateboarding, you should always wear a helmet and knee and elbow pads for protection.

Skateboard girl pro!

Elissa Streamer of the USA has won three gold medals in the women's street skate category of the X Games. She started skateboarding at the age of 12.

WORLD'S LONGEST RAMP JUMP

According to the Guinness Book of World Records, the longest skateboard ramp jump was performed by professional skateboarder Danny Way at the 2004 X Games in Los Angeles, California. Way jumped an astonishing 24m!

◆ *Wagner Ramos is a professional skateboarder, which means he skates for money, not just for fun!*

Skateboard dude

Wagner Ramos, a 16-year-old skateboarder from Brazil, was chosen as best all-round athlete at the 2006 **Gravity Games** in the USA. Friends describe him as a "mellow fellow" who loves music.

A SCOOTER is a close relative of the skateboard. It is essentially a skateboard with a long handle and two narrow wheels similar to rollerblade wheels. Razor scooters are so-named because their shape looks a little like an old-fashioned barber's razor – the kind with a blade that flicks out from a long handle.

Mopeds and foot bikes

'Scooter' is also a term for a moped – a two-wheeled, motorcycle-like vehicle popular in Italy. Mopeds are ideal for getting about narrow city streets. Another kind of scooter is the foot bike – a bicycle with a flat, scooter-like platform in the centre instead of a seat and pedals. The rider pushes the bike along with one foot.

HOW TO RIDE A RAZOR SCOOTER

To ride a razor scooter, place one foot on the flat part of the scooter and use your other foot to push the scooter along. Alternatively, place your second foot behind the first and glide! Use the T-shaped handle bar to steer.

Motorized scooters

Some motorized scooters look just like razor scooters, but have small engines at the back. Others, called mini scooters, stand just under 1m tall and feature T-shaped handlebars. Some people want to ban certain types of motorized scooter because they can travel at up to 64kph, but offer no protection for the rider if they collide with another vehicle.

◄ Foot bike races take place either on roads or special tracks. Competitors can race for individual medals, or as part of a team in relay races.

SCOOTING

To stop a razor scooter, you simply press down with your foot on the brake that extends over the back wheel.

RAZORS AND ROLLERBLADES

A razor scooter has narrow wheels like those of rollerblades (above). Some scooter riders have learned to be just as agile as rollerbladers, and can perform amazing stunts at skate park contests.

MOUNTAIN BIKING

IF YOU LIKE riding your bike, and you like **hiking** in the woods or along rough tracks, then the chances are you will like mountain biking. Mountain biking is just what it sounds like – riding a special bike up and down hills or mountains. Some people bike in summer on the same mountains that are used for skiing in winter, when they are covered in snow. People also bike through woods, across deserts or on other types of rough **terrain**.

WHERE TO BIKE

Wondering where to mountain bike? Ask in your local library for information about woodland trails that are open to mountain bikes, or find out where your nearest mountain-biking group meets.

Special gear

Mountain biking requires a special bike with fat, bumpy tyres that can grip the **trail** and keep the bike stable and upright on rocks, roots or muddy ground. Like other bikes, mountain bikes also have gears, which let you get more power from the bike (in low gears) or more speed (in higher gears).

▶ *On a smooth road surface, a mountain bike needs more pedal-power to go the same speed as a road bike. This is because its knobbly tyres provide such good grip that they slow the bike down.*

SAFETY FIRST

As with many extreme sports, a helmet and knee and elbow pads will protect your head, knees and elbows from falls or flying rocks. In the extreme version of mountain biking, called **bicycle motocross (BMX)**, participants wear full-body padded suits, special protective gloves, goggles and shoes that grip the pedals. The full-face helmet worn by BMX riders closely resembles those used for skiing, riding motorcycles or **snowmobiling**.

OLYMPIC GAMES

Cross-country mountain biking was first officially included in the Olympics in 1996. That year, Bart Brentjens of the Netherlands took the gold medal. He also won an Olympic bronze in 2004.

Practice is an important part of mountain biking. You'll need to practise braking, especially if you are riding up and down hills or steep slopes.

Mt. biking

Be prepared!

Muddy or rocky trails can take it out of both you and your bike, so it is important to carry a few essentials with you. Take a full water bottle, so you don't get dehydrated, and a repair kit, in case you need to repair your bike in some remote place. The kit should include a multi-tool designed to repair bikes, a patch kit for fixing flat tyres and a mini pump.

➥ *In a motocross race, all riders start at the same time, and the first biker across the finish line wins.*

TRIATHLONS

In three-part, multi-sport events called triathlons, racing bikes along the roads usually forms one part of the race. But some special triathlons, often called XTerras, involve mountain biking instead. Participants swim in a lake, go mountain biking and then run to the finish.

Motocross and BMX

Motocross is related to mountain biking, but motorcycles are ridden instead of bicycles. Powered by petrol, the bikes can go much faster than mountain bikes, and cover longer distances. BMX bikes are pedal-powered racing bikes. They have smaller wheels than mountain bikes and are designed for strength.

HOLD TIGHT!

Motocross is very demanding: riders must control a heavy motorcycle while driving as fast as possible on a rough and bumpy course.

➤ *Mountain biking is a great form of exercise. Pedalling uses the muscles of your legs and hips, and steering the bike strengthens your arm muscles.*

Brake power

A mountain bike's brakes (called **cantilever** brakes) are more like motorcycle brakes than a road bike's **caliper** brakes. Cantilever brakes give you more control over how fast you come down a hill. Many experienced mountain bikers descend using a technique called feathering – gently squeezing and releasing the brake. Feathering can prevent the wheels from locking. If your wheels lock, you can go into a spin, which could cause an injury.

I·M·B·A
International Mountain
Bicycling Association

IMBA-UK

The International Mountain Bicycling Association (UK) (IMBA-UK) is dedicated to preserving and expanding trails for mountain biking. Its members ride on trails all over the world. Check it out at: www.imba-uk.com

SNORKELLING

SNORKELLING is a fun and easy extreme sport, providing you can swim! All you need to get started is a mask, a snorkel and flippers. You can snorkel in a fresh lake, exploring the shoreline for tadpoles and frogs, or in the sea, where you might see brightly coloured fish swimming past.

FLIPPERS

To swim with flippers, you'll need to learn how to do the 'flutter kick'. This involves kicking rapidly back and forth with legs straight (no bending at the knees!).

Fun with flippers

Breathing through a snorkel and swimming with a mask and flippers all at the same time may take a little while to learn. If you are a beginner, first try swimming with just the flippers to get used to the feel of them. You'll be able to go really fast!

The mask and tube

A snorkelling mask is fun to wear because it lets you see under water, while keeping the water out of your eyes. Breathing through the mouthpiece and the tube of the snorkel takes practice. Don't forget to hold your breath if you dive under water, as water will go down the tube! You will need to blow the water back out of the tube when you come back up to the surface.

◀ The rubber rim of a snorkel mask fits tightly round the face so that water is unable to get in.

Scuba diving

Scuba diving is a sport for adults. Wearing special equipment, scuba divers can swim deep under the sea, and can stay under water for long periods. Sometimes they are hired to look for treasure or shipwrecks.

Diving deep

Scuba divers carry **oxygen tanks** on their backs for underwater breathing, and wear wetsuits, rubber gloves and zip-up rubber boots. They may wear a headlamp, too, as deep in the ocean it's very dark!

WORLD RECORD

In June 2005, South African scuba diver Nuno Gomes set a new world record in diving. Gomes dived to a depth of 318.25m, a depth almost equal to the height of the Eiffel Tower in Paris. For more world records, check out: www.guinnessworldrecords.com

➤ *In shallow coastal waters, a snorkeller can see all kinds of wonderful things, such as these starfish off the coast of Honeymoon Island, Palau, in the Pacific Ocean.*

KITING

WHEN YOU think of kite flying, you may think of a simple diamond-shaped piece of plastic, a few wooden sticks and a ball of string. But kiting gets far more extreme than that! Competitive kite flying is growing in popularity in the UK, while in the USA, Germany, Japan and Thailand (among other countries) people fly giant kites more than 24m in length.

Kite varieties

There are many different types of kites, including single-string kites, which you may have flown in a field or on a beach; stunt kites, which are designed to do tricks or special manoeuvres; and power kites, which have enough power to pull surfers across the sea or **snowboarders** across a snowy plain.

STACK

STACK stands for Sport Team and Competitive Kiting, a UK organization that tries to bring together anyone who loves the sport of kiting. Its members compete in Individual, Pairs, Team and Trick-flying kite competitions all over the world.

Kiting is often done at the beach, where there is plenty of room to run and launch a kite, and often a good wind blowing in off the sea to lift it.

WORLD'S SMALLEST AND BIGGEST KITES

Kites range from very small to huge. According to the Guinness Book of World Records, the smallest kite ever flown measured 10 x 8mm – roughly the size of a pea. This miniature kite was flown by Nobuhiko Yoshizuni of Kyoto, Japan. In complete contrast, the MegaFlag, produced by a US company called Gomberg Kite Productions, measures 40 x 24m. That's bigger than most houses!

To do kitesurfing, you need to be skilled at flying kites, as well as being a strong swimmer.

Festivals and competitions

One easy way to become familiar with kiting is to visit a competition or festival. There are kite competitions for speed and design, and festivals that celebrate sport kites, **box kites**, foils (soft, semi-inflated kites used for kitesurfing and **snowkiting**) and deltas (arrow-shaped kites used for stunts). A major kiting event is held each year in the US capital, Washington, DC. It includes a kite design competition, judged on visual appeal and handling, and trick flying competitions.

Kitesurfing

In kitesurfing, you use a large kite to pull yourself across the water on a wakeboard. Experts are able to perform some amazing jumps.

SNOWKITING

Snowkiting is similar to kitesurfing, but instead combines a kite and a snowboard. Check out the Swiss Snowkiting School's website: www.snowkiting.ch (To get the English-language version, you'll need to click on 'english' in the black bar at the top of the homepage.)

SURFING

SURFING may have its roots in the ancient cultures of Polynesia and Tahiti. It was witnessed in the late 1770s by British explorer Captain James Cook, who came across the Hawaiian islands, where he saw the native people riding the waves on wooden boards. Today's boards, made from a special kind of **resin**-coated plastic, include surfboards, paipo (short boards) and round **skimmers**.

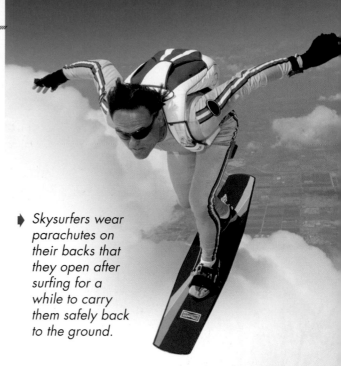

▶ Skysurfers wear parachutes on their backs that they open after surfing for a while to carry them safely back to the ground.

The biggest waves

Major surfing centres have sprung up along the Pacific and Atlantic coasts, which receive some of the world's biggest waves. Australia, California and Hawaii all have strong surfing communities. By some estimates there are 20 million surfers worldwide. The sport is exciting to watch, especially if you're seeing world-class surfers tackling the biggest waves the ocean can produce.

Take to the air

While surfing brings together a body, a board and a wave, skysurfing combines a body, a board and the air. Skysurfers jump from a plane and ride the air currents on a board strapped to their feet! Only highly trained professionals are able to do this sport.

SURF ART

Surfboard artist Drew Brophy of California is so well known among musicians and rocks stars that his painted surfboards sell for thousands of pounds. Drew says his designs are inspired by the ocean, surfing and nature.

Surfing vs. bodyboarding

Watching the world's best surfers and learning how to surf are two very different things! Learning the art of ocean surfing (or **windsurfing**, which adds a sail and apparatus to the board) requires time and patience. You may instead be drawn to bodyboarding – surfing while lying down on a 1-m long board (also called a boogie board). Or, on the beach, you might prefer to try out a skimmer – a round, thin board that you skim across the shallows and jump on to with both feet so that you can skid across the wet sand.

WORLD RECORD HOLDER

According to the Guinness Book of World Records, Mike Stewart of the USA has won nine world championships in bodyboarding, and 21 Pipeline titles. (Pipeline is a famous Hawaiian wave venue.)

After paddling out to sea lying on the board, a surfer has to get to his or her feet. Some people prefer to crouch first on one knee and make sure both feet are in the right position, before they stand up.

SURF LINGO

Surfing has a language and culture all of its own. In California, 'cooking' means a really good wave and 'noodled' means exhausted. 'Wipe out' means to fall off the board – which is when you don't want to meet a 'landlord' (a great white shark). 'Hang ten' is a trick in which you have all ten toes on the nose (front) of the board.

KNEEBOARDING and wakeboarding are great extreme sports for children, assuming you have access to the proper equipment, a good teacher, a snug life jacket and...a powerboat! In kneeboarding, you are pulled behind a boat while kneeling on a board. In wakeboarding, you are also pulled behind a boat, but you stand sideways on a specially designed board that resembles a snowboard.

Wakeboards have to be very strong to withstand the pounding they get as their riders jump them over the wake (waves) created behind a powerboat and land back on the water.

Waterskiing

Both kneeboarding and wakeboarding are related to waterskiing, in which you are pulled behind a powerboat while standing on wide, flat skis. Waterskiing has a long history in the USA, and it's an Olympic sport. Check it out at www.usawaterski.org

Barefoot waterskiing

Barefoot waterskiing involves skiing on water without skis! At the 2006 Barefoot Water Ski World Championships, Keith St. Onge became an overall gold medalist in the Men's **Slalom**, Tricks and Overall categories. He started waterskiing at the age of 10 and has had years of experience, so don't try any of his tricks at home!

When he's not barefoot waterskiing, Keith St. Onge likes cold-weather sports such as ice hockey and snow skiing.

KNEEBOARDING

Many children find kneeboarding easier than waterskiing, because instead of having to balance on two skis, you simply kneel on a large board and let the boat pull you along.

WATERSKIING VS. DOWNHILL (SNOW) SKIING

Waterskiing is different from **downhill skiing** in several ways. First, the skis used for waterskiing are wider. Secondly, you do not usually wear boots while waterskiing, as your feet need to release quickly if you take a tumble in the water. Thirdly, downhill skiers don't need to wear life jackets!

ROCK CLIMBING

ROCK CLIMBING is a fun and challenging sport that can be tackled outdoors on real rocks or inside on artificial climbing walls. The sport requires good upper body strength, because you use your arms to pull yourself up the surface you're climbing. All beginners wear a harness attached to ropes, which are designed to catch or stop you if you fall.

WHY CLIMB A MOUNTAIN?

What makes climbers want to climb mountains? As Sir Edmund Hillary, one of the first two men to reach the summit of Mount Everest, is reported to have said: "It is not the mountain we conquer, but ourselves." For more info on Mount Everest, visit: www.mounteverest.net

Indoor rock climbing

Indoor climbing walls feature handholds made from rubber or plastic that the climbers hold onto as they go up. But what goes up must come down – which is why the ropes are important. Once a climber reaches the top, the trained professional holding on to the ropes at the bottom can guide him or her safely down again.

Hiking and hill climbing

Like rock climbing, hiking and **hill climbing** take place on hills and mountains, but they use your leg muscles more than your arm muscles.

Rock climbers wear a padded harness, which loops around the waist and around each leg. Safety ropes attach to the harness.

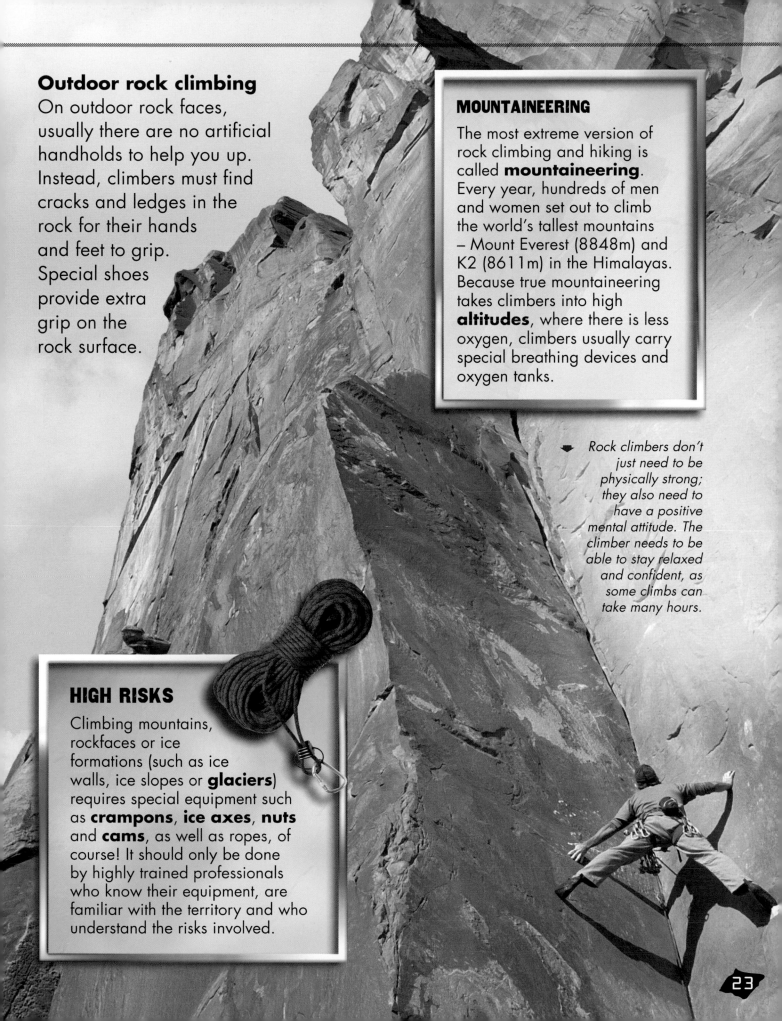

Outdoor rock climbing

On outdoor rock faces, usually there are no artificial handholds to help you up. Instead, climbers must find cracks and ledges in the rock for their hands and feet to grip. Special shoes provide extra grip on the rock surface.

MOUNTAINEERING

The most extreme version of rock climbing and hiking is called **mountaineering**. Every year, hundreds of men and women set out to climb the world's tallest mountains – Mount Everest (8848m) and K2 (8611m) in the Himalayas. Because true mountaineering takes climbers into high **altitudes**, where there is less oxygen, climbers usually carry special breathing devices and oxygen tanks.

➡ *Rock climbers don't just need to be physically strong; they also need to have a positive mental attitude. The climber needs to be able to stay relaxed and confident, as some climbs can take many hours.*

HIGH RISKS

Climbing mountains, rockfaces or ice formations (such as ice walls, ice slopes or **glaciers**) requires special equipment such as **crampons**, **ice axes**, **nuts** and **cams**, as well as ropes, of course! It should only be done by highly trained professionals who know their equipment, are familiar with the territory and who understand the risks involved.

KAYAKING

IF YOU like the water, kayaking may be the extreme sport for you. A kayak is a lightweight, enclosed boat that you can paddle on lakes, rivers or the sea using a two-sided paddle. To move the boat, you dip the paddle in the water on each side of the kayak, one side at a time, and pull or push it through the water. Some kayaks are designed for one person, others for two.

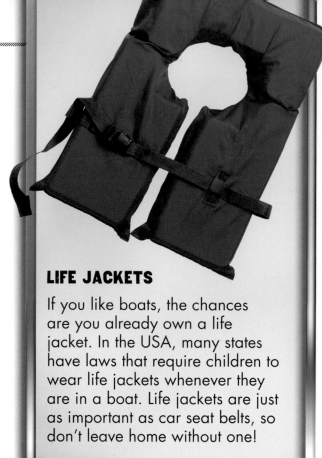

LIFE JACKETS

If you like boats, the chances are you already own a life jacket. In the USA, many states have laws that require children to wear life jackets whenever they are in a boat. Life jackets are just as important as car seat belts, so don't leave home without one!

Splashing about!

Kayaking is closely related to **canoeing** and **rafting**, both of which are fun boating sports for children. In the UK, kids can also enjoy sailing and racing Toppers – small, single-person sailing boats. In Canada, the USA, parts of South America and New Zealand, small boats called Sunfish are popular.

Sunfish are a great sailing boat for children because they're lightweight and easy enough for one person to sail by themselves.

White water kayaking

The most extreme version of kayaking is white water kayaking. You need to be highly trained for this sport. The aim is to manoeuvre a kayak through the rough and unpredictable 'white water' of **rapids** in a fast-flowing river. The sport is exciting (even scary) to watch, as it can be a dangerous activity and is definitely not for beginners!

WHITE WATER RAFTING

For the most extreme version of rafting, called white water rafting, you'll need a trained instructor, a large **inflatable boat** and a group of friends. The aim is to paddle the boat along a fast-flowing river. Everyone wears life jackets and helmets in case they fall in.

White water kayakers can choose the difficulty of the river they want to paddle on. A Class VI (six) river is considered the most difficult and dangerous to navigate. A class I is the easiest.

MULTI-SPORT EVENTS

MULTI-SPORT events are just what they sound like: sporting events that combine multiple sports. There are many different types of multi-sport events. A 'triathlon' combines swimming, cycling and running ('tri' is from the Greek word for three). The winter sport of 'biathlon' combines cross-country skiing and rifle shooting (although the term 'biathlon' can be used to describe any two-sport event). In a 'duathlon', an athlete runs, bikes, and then runs again.

TRIATHLON WORLD CHAMPION

Tim Don of the UK won the men's elite division of the 2006 triathlon World Championships, held in Switzerland. Don finished the 1.5km swim, 40km bike ride and 10km run in one hour, 51 minutes and 32 seconds.

The swimming part of a junior triathlon can take place outdoors in a lake or indoors in a pool.

All-round skills

You may be good at swimming, biking and running, but triathlon requires another skill, too. A triathlete must also be able to change clothes and/or equipment quickly and efficiently at 'transitions' – the time between stages. You will need three sets of equipment: goggles and cap for swimming; bike and helmet for biking; and proper shoes for running. Keeping it all organized is very important, because the quicker your transition time, the faster your finishing time!

TRANSITION AREA

The transition area is the place the athlete returns to after each leg of the triathlon. After swimming, for instance, the professional competitor must take off his or her goggles and cap and quickly put on cycling shorts, gloves, shoes and helmet.

➡ After completing the swim, triathletes run over to their bikes, where they put on their shoes and helmet before setting off cycling.

➡ Some athletes wear specially adapted tri suits, which look like swimming costumes, for all three stages, including the run.

Sail and run

Multi-sport events take many different forms. In the UK, the Three Peaks Yacht Race combines yachting (626km) and mountain running (115.8km), plus a little cycling (30km). Competitors sail from Barmouth in west Wales to Fort William in north-west Scotland. On the way they climb to the summits of Britain's three highest peaks: Snowdon, Scafell Pike and Ben Nevis.

Choice of events

Each year in Okalahoma City, USA, competitors can compete in an event called a half REDMAN (swim 1.9km, bike 90km and run 21km); a full REDMAN (swim 3.8km, bike 180.2km and run 42.2km – the distance of a full **marathon**); or do the Aqua Bike event (swimming and cycling).

KID STAR

Sara McLarty has been the US IronKids champion four times. She lives in Colorado Springs, USA, where the Olympic triathlon team trains. Sara first became an IronKids champion at the age of 10!

➡ Before attempting the swimming portion of the race, many triathletes do some warm-up exercises and then stretch their arms to give their muscles greater flexibility.

BODY MARKINGS

To keep track of them all, multi-sport competitors are given a number which is marked on their bodies (with permanent ink), attached to their bikes and pinned to the fronts of their shirts for the running portion of the race.

The run is sometimes the hardest part of the triathlon, as your legs are tired from biking and your whole body is tired from swimming!

Strong as iron!

One of the most famous triathlon events is called the Ironman (in which women also compete). Competitors in this gruelling event swim, bike and run the same distances as a full REDMAN. Children can compete in their own version of the race called IronKids. Junior triathlon distances might include a 125m swim, an 8km bike ride and a 2.5km run.

GLOSSARY

altitude The height of a landmass or mountain above sea level.

bicycle motocross (BMX) Racing special mountain bikes over rough ground around a hilly course.

box kite A classic type of kite in the shape of a rectangular box.

caliper brakes A type of bicycle brake found on road bikes. Caliper brakes attach above the wheel and squeeze together on either side of the wheel rim to slow the bike down.

cams (mountaineering) Cams are grooved, wheel-like devices with handles that you insert into cracks in the rock and attach your climbing ropes to. If they are placed at frequent intervals up the rockface, they will stop you falling very far.

canoeing Paddling a canoe – a long, narrow boat with pointed ends like a kayak, but with an open top.

cantilever brakes A type of bicycle brake found on mountain bikes. Cantilever brakes attach next to the wheel and are more powerful than caliper brakes.

coach Someone who trains or instructs an individual or a team in a particular sport, and helps them to improve their skills.

crampon An iron plate with spikes that you fix to your boots to give you grip when walking on ice.

downhill skiing A winter sport in which participants use a pair of skis to glide or race down a snow-covered mountain.

glacier A large, frozen river of ice moving very slowly down a valley.

Gravity Games An annual competition for extreme sporting events, such as snowboarding and skateboarding.

hiking To walk, climb, explore and/or travel along paths and trails. Hiking trails are often found in places such as mountainous areas, forests and along the coast.

hill climbing To climb or hike up hills, sometimes holding long poles for support.

ice axe An axe used by mountain-climbers for cutting footholds in the ice. One end is hooked and has a serrated edge (like a bread knife).

inflatable boat A boat that is filled with air in order to float.

marathon A road race covering a distance of 42.2km.

motocross Racing a motorcycle over rough or hilly terrain.

mountaineering The sport of walking, hiking and rock climbing up mountains, often over snow and ice. It is also sometimes known as Alpinism, particularly in Europe.

nuts (mountaineering) Metal wedges that, like cams, you insert into cracks in the rock, and attach ropes to, to stop you falling very far.

oxygen tank A tank that holds oxygen and is used when swimming underwater (as in scuba diving) or mountaineering in high altitudes (as on Mount Everest).

rafting To ride an inflatable raft down a river, often over rapids.

rapids Fast-moving parts of a river, where the water tumbles over and between rocks. Rapids are also known as 'white water', because all the bubbles make the water look white.

resin A liquid substance that hardens; artificial resins are used in some plastics. Natural resin is found in the gum of some trees.

scuba The letters 'scuba' stand for Self Contained Underwater Breathing Apparatus. It is the name given to part of the gear used by underwater divers.

skimmer A round, thin board about half the length and thickness of a surfboard, and with no fin on the bottom. You ride a skimmer across wet sand and towards incoming waves.

slalom To zigzag between obstacles in certain sports, such as skiing.

snowboarder Someone who rides a long, flat board down ski slopes or in terrain parks.

snowkiting A sport in which you stand on a snowboard and are pulled along by a kite, which is powered by the wind.

snowmobiling A sport in which you race a motorized sledge with skis and a caterpillar track across ice and snow.

terrain Land used for activities such as mountain biking or hiking.

trail A path used for sports such as walking, hiking, mountain biking and horse riding. In snowboarding and downhill skiing, 'trail' refers to the path that takes you from the top of the mountain to the bottom.

triathlon A multi-sport event that combines swimming, biking (road or mountain) and running.

windsurfing A sport that involves standing up on a board similar to a surfboard, but equipped with a sail, and moving across the water using the power of the wind.

X Games An international competition similar to the Olympics that includes sports such as skateboarding.

WEBSITES
Mountain biking www.imba-uk.com
Snowkiting www.snowkiting.ch
Waterskiing www.usawaterski.org
Rock climbing (Mount Everest) www.mounteverest.net
General www.guinnessworldrecords.com

Index